L I S T E N E R ' S

mood

Winter
Landscape

Winter Landscapes

Winter may seem like a bleak time, a season full of ice and cold, but it also has a way of transforming a landscape into something rich and magical. A thick blanket of freshly fallen snow can make us suddenly aware of the natural beauty around us: almost as if we were seeing the world for the first time. This collection gathers together the most evocative descriptions of winter in the history of classical music, from Vivaldi's dramatic "Winter," to Mozart's dashing "Sleigh Ride," Tchaikovsky's "Waltz of the Snowflakes," and Debussy's delightful "The Snow is Dancing." *Winter Landscapes* will allow you to enjoy the unique experience of winter—without the frozen fingers!

THE LISTENER'S GUIDE — WHAT THE SYMBOLS MEAN

THE COMPOSERS
Their lives... their loves.. their legacies...

THE MUSIC
Explanation... analysis... interpretation...

THE INSPIRATION
How works of genius came to be written

THE BACKGROUND
People, places, and events linked to the music

© MCMXCVIII IMP AB   In Classical Mood™   IMP AB, produced under license by IMP Inc.   Printed in China. US P 2201 12 047

Contents

ANTONIO VIVALDI *1678–1741*

The Four Seasons

OPUS 8, NO.4: WINTER

A Venetian winter can be harsh, as this delightful musical portrait evokes, with its whistling winds and much stamping of feet. Vivaldi's famous work *The Four Seasons* shows each season in all its different moods, but it is best enjoyed from the sanctuary of a warm house! As with the other "*Seasons*," the composer prefaced the music with a sonnet: "To shiver icily in the freezing dark in the teeth of a cruel wind, to stamp your feet all the time, so chilled that your teeth chatter. To remain in quiet contentment by the fireside while outside the rain pours in torrents…To step forth strongly, fall to the ground, and again run boldly on the ice until it cracks and breaks…such is winter."

ART AND NATURE

From around 1000 AD until the beginning of the 16th century, the prime inspiration in European arts was Christianity. But, as the ideas of the Renaissance began to take hold, it was Nature that artists turned to for inspiration. Vivaldi's *The Four Seasons* and its immediate popularity reflects this progressive cultural shift. Around 1730, the French philosopher Montesquieu noted of English life, "If anyone mentions religion, people begin to laugh." The English poet Thomas Gray, crossing the Alps in 1739, claimed that the awesome mountains were "pregnant with religion and poetry." Nature, increasingly the subject of art and science, was now even an object of worship.

Nature's awe and art-inspiring Alps.

VENETIAN REVELRY

The Venetians have always loved ceremonies and spectacle, particularly when they have the chance to join in. The annual winter carnival in Venice—which still takes place—was almost a pagan event, when people wore masks and sexual license was commonplace. Church events were also an excuse for public enjoyment. When St. Peter Orseolo was canonized, the celebrations went on for three days. However, there was a darker, crueller side to

Venetian life. Between 1741 and 1762, for example, an estimated 73,000 people were either executed or condemned to the galleys.

KEY NOTES

Although he was a priest, Vivaldi was not the most pious of men. Perhaps to cover his lack of religious dedication, he frequently headed his works with the motto "LD" (Laus Deo or "Praise be to God") or "LDBMDA," for Laus Deo Beataeque Mariae Deiparae ("Praise be to God and the blessed Virgin Mary") Amen.

NIKOLAI RIMSKY-KORSAKOV *1844–1908*

The Snow Maiden

DANCE OF THE TUMBLERS

This exuberant dance from Rimsky-Korsakov's rarely performed opera *The Snow Maiden* centers around a group of energetic tumblers (acrobats) performing before the Tzar. They are celebrating the end of winter, and the constant energy of the dance is clear from the scurrying strings which seldom let up—except to take their part in playing the perky melody. The brass section also joins in the fun, although occasionally its snarling has a more sober, almost menacing edge to it. Such dark moments are soon dispelled as the woodwind and string instruments resume their ebullient business. The "Dance of the Tumblers" is as full of surprises as the breathtaking formations of the acrobats it vividly depicts. Even in an age when Russian music was noted for its color and invention, Rimsky-Korsakov's score stands out as one of the very best.

THE OPERA

The heroine of the opera *The Snow Maiden* is Snegurochka—the daughter of King Frost and Fairy Spring. Because her heart is made of ice, she is doomed to die if it ever melts, and so she must live in a dark woodland. She becomes attracted to a shepherd, Lehl, but he is in love with a girl named Kupava. Then Kupava's fiancé Mizgir falls in love with Snegurochka. The Tzar is asked to mediate, but he too becomes captivated by her beauty. Finally, the confused Snegurochka begs her mother, Fairy Spring, to warm her heart so that she can love Mizgir. But just before their wedding, she is touched by a ray of sun and melts. The distraught and crazed Mizgir drowns himself.

THE PLAY

The Snow Maiden is based on the play *Snegurochka* by Alexander Nikolaevich Ostrovsky (*right*), one of the foremost 19th-century Russian dramatists. Based on an ancient Russian fairytale, *Snegurochka* was unlike most of Ostrovsky's other works, which consisted mainly of historical dramas and social comedies. Ostrovsky worked for a while as a clerk at the Moscow juvenile court and in 1850, his first comic play, *The Bankrupt*, provoked an outcry by exposing the problem of fraudulent bankruptcies. In a distinguished career, Ostrovsky went on to found the Society of Russian Playwrights and become artistic director of the Moscow Imperial Theater.

KEY NOTES

It was Tchaikovsky who wrote the incidental music for the first performance of Ostrovsky's play Snegurochka, *in 1873. The music proved much more successful than the play itself, and Tchaikovsky planned to expand it into an opera. However, Rimsky-Korsakov got there first.*

CLAUDE DEBUSSY *1862–1918*

Children's Corner

THE SNOW IS DANCING

ebussy dedicated his *Children's Corner* suite to his baby daughter Claude-Emma: "To my dear little Chou-Chou, with her father's affectionate apologies for what follows." Such gentle irony and affection is evident throughout the suite's six movements, which evoke a child's world. The fourth movement, "The Snow is Dancing," magically conjures up the winter scene that a young girl might watch through a window. Appropriately, the musical means are simple. A constant, light chatter of notes, suggesting snowflakes, runs throughout the piece, sometimes disjointed, at other times smooth and rippling. The note patterns change constantly, reflecting the ever-varied dance of the snowflakes, before spiralling upwards to a final, gentle flurry.

DEBUSSY AND CHOU-CHOU

Although not overly fond of children, Debussy adored his daughter Chou-Chou (*left*). Born in 1905, when the composer was troubled by illness, debt and scandal, she became the joy of his life. The singer Maggie Teyte, who performed in Debussy's opera *Pelléas et Mélisande* soon after Chou-Chou's birth, found the composer cold and consumed with anger. She noted, however, that "he showed another and more pleasant side of his nature when he was with Chou-Chou." Having a child also allowed Debussy to express his love of childlike things, such as the circus and puppets. His friend and biographer René Peter recalled, "Even the piano sometimes became...an arena for his crazy jokes."

HUNGARIAN BLUES

In 1910, Debussy was invited to undertake a series of piano recitals throughout the Austro-Hungarian Empire, a project he disliked but undertook for the money. In Budapest, a concert including the *Children's Corner* suite was performed before an audience of 1,500 people. Despite this, Debussy remained unimpressed by the Hungarians. Budapest, he said, was a city "where you get a surfeit of Brahms and Puccini, and where the officers have bosoms like women and the women bosoms like officers!"

The magnificent city of Budapest held few charms for Debussy.

KEY NOTES

The English titles of the Children's Corner suite reflect the language Debussy's daughter was picking up from her English governess. There was a great vogue for all things English at that time in Paris, and children were often dressed in English clothes.

SERGEI PROKOFIEV *1891–1953*

Winter Bonfire

DEPARTURE, SNOW OUTSIDE THE WINDOW, AND WALTZ ON ICE

Winter Bonfire, a symphonic suite for children, is based on verses written by Samuel Marshak, a popular children's author. It tells of an outing by a group of Young Pioneers (Soviet children between the ages of ten and 14) to the winter countryside one Sunday afternoon. "Departure," the first movement, describes the train journey there. Even with no knowledge of the story, the throb of the train is clear—simply but vividly depicted by a repeating pattern in strings and percussion. Brass and wind instruments send out jubilant calls and a jaunty theme soon appears. The Pioneers are clearly in high spirits.

SNOW OUTSIDE THE WINDOW

This second movement conjures up a picture of peaceful reverie. Perhaps the Pioneers are in awe of the serenity of the winter landscape. Certainly there are no signs of games or frolicking outside in the snow. It opens with a simple, plaintive tune on the oboe which is taken up by strings and then a horn. A more lopsided, comical melody then appears, but the opening mood is soon re-established as the movement draws to a serene and peaceful close.

WALTZ ON ICE

Prokofiev produces a swinging, lyrical tune for the Pioneers to skate to, full of quirky twists and turns that presumably mimic the activity of the skaters on the ice. This carefree music is rounded off with a jubilant finish. *Winter Bonfire* has five more movements. The fourth movement is "The Bonfire" itself. The fifth, "Pioneer Gathering," is set around the bonfire and includes a boys' chorus. Two further movements—"Winter Evening" and "Marching Song"—follow, before the train music from the beginning is heard again for the Pioneers' "Return."

FRIENDS IN ADVERSITY

One of Prokofiev's closest friends, and a man who had a great influence over his career, was Nikolai Myaskovsky (*far right*, with Prokofiev in 1941). Myaskovsky was also a composer, and for many years a professor at the Moscow Conservatory. It was he who stage-managed Prokofiev's return to Russia, first for a tour in 1927, then permanently in 1936. (Ironically, Myaskowsky was one of those who advised Prokofiev to leave Russia in 1918.) Both composers fell victim to Stalin's paranoia: in 1948 their music was condemned as unpatriotic. They managed to continue working (Prokofiev wrote *Winter Bonfire* in 1949) but, broken in health if not in spirit, neither had long to live—Myaskovsky died in 1950, three years before Prokofiev.

THE PIONEERS

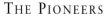

The Soviet Pioneers were founded in 1922 as a revolutionary replacement for the Scout Movement. Those who joined had to take the Pioneer oath: to respect truth, honesty and patriotism. They were then entitled to wear a red

neckerchief, with three corners representing the unity of the Pioneers, the Komsomol (the All-Union Leninist Communist Union of Youth) and the Communist Party. A Pioneer's duties included teaching younger children about communism and morality.

KEY NOTES

The happy nature of Winter Bonfire betrays nothing of the fact that when Prokofiev came to write it in 1949 he was a sick man. Confined to hospital after falling down some stairs and suffering a concussion, he was only allowed by his doctors to work for 20 minutes a day, though he would often surreptitiously break this strict rule.

TRACK 5

PYOTR TCHAIKOVSKY *1840–1893*

The Nutcracker

OPUS 71: WALTZ OF THE SNOWFLAKES

This waltz comes at the end of Act I of the ballet. The young girl Clara dreams that the nutcracker she was given as a Christmas present is transformed into a prince. He invites her to go with him to the Kingdom of Sweets, and on the way, they enter a magical, snow-covered forest, where they watch the swirling, dancing snowflakes. The waltz opens with a light theme tossed around by the flute— very much like snowflakes that are blown about in the wind—before the music whirls to an emphatic climax.

DOUBLE ACT

"Waltz of the Snowflakes" was the favorite part of the Imperial Ballet production of *The Nutcracker*, in 1892. It was one of the few scenes on which Tchaikovsky and Lev Ivanov, the choreographer, were free to work without following the detailed plans drawn up by their boss, Petipa.

KEY NOTES

Marius Petipa was chief ballet master of the Imperial Ballet in St. Petersburg and Moscow, from 1869 to 1903. Petipa made the Imperial Ballet the greatest ballet company of its day.

WOLFGANG AMADEUS MOZART
1756–1791

K605, No.3:
SLEIGH RIDE

Sleigh rides, complete with jangling bells and post horns, were very popular with the winter court in 18th-century Vienna. When Mozart was commissioned to write *Three German Dances* for the court in 1791, he included a sleigh ride in the trio, or central section, of the third dance. The dance opens with a simple, forthright theme before the sleigh bells start. A suitably graceful melody follows, in complete contrast to the previous music, and the two post horns join in, calling and answering each other. All of this is then repeated before the post horns give their final resounding call. The magical effect of such instruments can easily be imagined, the sound cutting through the cold night air as the Viennese nobles ride their sleighs through the snow-covered city.

MOZART'S LAST YEAR

The year 1791 was amazingly fruitful for Mozart. He was less troubled by debts than in the recent past, and his wife Constanze gave birth to a son, only the second of their six children to survive childbirth. Mozart also produced his last two operas, *La Clemenza di Tito* and "The Magic Flute." The latter was produced with his old friend Emanuel Schikaneder, who also played Papageno, the bird-man (*below right*). Sadly, Mozart was suffering from increasingly poor health and was fearful about his ability to write a "magic" opera. He need not have worried: the work was an instant success, recorded in history as one of his masterpieces. He also wrote his sublime *Clarinet Concerto* that year and began work on the *Requiem*—his final, unfinished work. By the end of November, this magnificent outpouring took its toll. Within three weeks, he was dead.

A LITTLE LIGHT MUSIC

Mozart was often called on to produce short dance pieces, particularly for balls during the winter months. It was a task he enjoyed, even though he was not always well paid. In the winter of 1790–91, he wrote more than 30 such pieces, including the *Three German Dances*. He often included novelty effects in his lighter music, such as impressions of a hurdy-gurdy, many of which display a delightful rustic simplicity.

The itinerant hurdy-gurdy man

K E Y   N O T E S

Mozart loved parties and social occasions. Indeed, his desire to be part of the Viennese social scene led him to live beyond his means. He was an enthusiastic dancer, and a great lover of fancy dress balls.

FRÉDÉRIC CHOPIN *1810–1849*

Étude in A Minor

OPUS 25, NO.11: WINTER WIND

This is one of many *études*, or studies, which Chopin wrote exploring and testing different aspects of piano technique. The *Étude in A Minor* tests the agility of the pianist's right hand to its utmost while the left hand, for the most part, hammers out the stark theme which is announced at the beginning. Chopin did not give the work a name, and it was not intended to be a descriptive piece, but the perpetual motion of the right hand, sweeping up and down the keyboard, and the bleak accompaniment earned it the nickname "Winter Wind." It is a relentless piece, restless and forceful, the constantly reiterated theme reinforcing the cold inevitability of fate. A more desolate, wintry piece than this would be hard to find.

THE TEACHER IN PARIS

Chopin composed this *Étude in A Minor* in 1834, three years after he settled in Paris. Almost immediately after his arrival in the French capital, he became sought after by the aristocracy as a piano teacher, something which brought him more financial reward than personal fulfillment. Many of his pupils were high-born ladies seeking to perfect their social accomplishments. When he found serious students, however, he was conscientious. He even applied for military exemption for one, Adolph Gutmann, who unfortunately achieved very little musically. Perhaps his most notable student was Princess Marcelline Czartoryska (*above*), a fine interpreter of his music and also a close friend.

Chopin's students gather 'round to hear the master play.

THE MAN AND THE MYTH

For most of his life, Chopin (*right*) was plagued by weakness and ill-health. For many years, he suffered from tuberculosis, the disease that eventually killed him. Chopin's poor health helped to foster an image of the composer as a delicate, frail figure, dominated by those around him. This is a long way from the truth. Although physically weak, he was emotionally resilient and full of pride and passion, an aspect of his character that is reflected in his many vigorous compositions.

KEY NOTES

As well as completing seven of his second set of études in 1834, Chopin also produced his Grande Valse Brilliante, the Fantasia on Polish Airs and "The Krakowiak" Rondo. The year also saw the publication of Adam Mickiewicz's Polish epic Pan Tadeusz, which greatly influenced Chopin.

GEORGE FRIDERIC HANDEL *1685–1759*

Messiah

PASTORAL SYMPHONY

Within this short orchestral piece, Handel sets the scene of a peaceful country landscape, with shepherds tending their sheep. Gently lilting strings glide over long-held bass notes, the only ruffle on the surface being occasional trills. "Symphony" here is used in the 17th-century sense of "sinfonia," which could be an instrumental introduction to a vocal piece. Although short, the "Pastoral Symphony" has a vital function in *Messiah*. Preceding it is a prophecy of the coming of Jesus, while immediately after it comes the nativity celebration. This piece separates the two, and foretells what is to come.

FROM OPERA TO ORATORIO

After Handel (*left*) came to London in 1710, he soon established himself as the local master of Italian opera. He enjoyed consistent success for more than 20 years, but by the 1730s, it was clear that public tastes were changing, and he turned increasingly to oratorio. In late 1741, he was invited to produce a season in Dublin, where he performed a number of his smaller works and gave organ recitals. At that time, he had been working on his oratorio *Samson* but, possibly because he thought it too ambitious, he chose not to introduce it in Dublin. Instead, in 1742, he gave the premiere of his oratorio *Messiah* there, in the new concert hall before an audience of 700 people. It was a sensation.

MESSIAH AND THE FOUNDLING HOSPITAL

In 1750, Handel was asked to provide a musical performance for the opening of the chapel in the Hospital for the Maintenance and Education of Exposed and Deserted Young Children (*below*), in London. He put on *Messiah*, to enormous success. He subsequently bequeathed a copy of the work to the hospital, which later became the Thomas Coram Foundation in what is now London's Bloomsbury district. It still holds the manuscript, while nearby, Handel Street commemorates the composer.

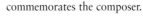

KEY NOTES

The first performance of the oratorio *Messiah* was so eagerly anticipated that advertisements were placed asking ladies who were attending to come without hoop-framed skirts, and gentlemen to come without their swords, so allowing more people to crowd into the hall.

EMILE WALDTEUFEL *1837–1915*

The Skaters' Waltz

Waldteufel wrote this, the most popular of his many waltzes, in 1882, when he was enjoying a revival in his musical fortunes. It paints a vivid picture of a delightful winter scene, with skaters gliding effortlessly and gracefully across the ice—or trying to. At the start, wind and strings call to each other, sliding up and down, before the main melody is heard distantly under shimmering strings. At the start of the waltz proper, the famous tune is heard immediately, closely followed by a second, slightly more mischievous one. Soon skyrocketing strings followed by musical bumps suggest that not everyone is managing to skim successfully across the ice. Melodies continue to crowd in on each other, competing in their elegance before the original tune returns and the piece heads to its joyful conclusion.

IMPERIAL FAVORITE

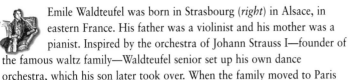

Emile Waldteufel was born in Strasbourg (*right*) in Alsace, in eastern France. His father was a violinist and his mother was a pianist. Inspired by the orchestra of Johann Strauss I—founder of the famous waltz family—Waldteufel senior set up his own dance orchestra, which his son later took over. When the family moved to Paris in 1842, the young Emile studied piano at the Conservatoire and earned a living testing pianos, giving lessons and playing at private musical evenings. In 1865, he was appointed court pianist by the Empress Eugénie and soon graduated to conducting at state balls throughout the country. However, Waldteufel lost this powerful patron when France lost its monarchy in the aftermath of the Franco-Prussian War of 1870–71. For a while he sank into relative obscurity. His fortunes revived after he met the Prince of Wales (the future King Edward VII), and his music, performed by his Orchestre Waldteufel, became extremely popular in Britain. Waldteufel retired in 1899, and died 16 years later in Paris.

DANCE CRAZE

Nineteenth-century France was a place of political turmoil. Nevertheless, or possibly as a result of this, the French took their pleasures seriously, and public dances were extravagant occasions. It was not unusual to find 3,000 people at a single event. The most popular dance was the waltz, and Emile Waldteufel was prominent among the many musicians feeding an insatiable desire for new music.

A masked ball at the Paris Opéra.

ALSACE, THE FOOTBALL OF EUROPE

Waldteufel's birthplace of Strasbourg is the capital of Alsace (*right*) which, together with its neighboring province of Lorraine, has long been the center of territorial disputes between France and Germany. A region rich in iron ore, various parts of the area were ruled by the Holy Roman Empire, France and German duchies until France assumed control in the 17th century. The area then became German after the Franco-Prussian War of 1870–1871, before reverting once more to France under the Treaty of Versailles in 1919. In 1940, the Nazis, following their occupation of France, proclaimed the region to be German, though their eventual defeat saw Alsace-Lorraine return to French rule yet again.

EMPRESS EUGÉNIE

The Empress Eugénie, who took a great interest in the career of Waldteufel, was the wife of Napoleon III. The daughter of a Spanish noble and granddaughter of a Scottish wine-merchant, she married Napoleon in 1853. She was famed for her beauty and presided over the most glittering court in Europe. After the fall of Napoleon in 1870, the family fled to England, where Eugénie lived for another 50 years, first in Kent, then in Farnborough, Hampshire.

Eugénie and Napoleon III enjoy a sleigh ride in Paris's Bois de Boulogne.

KEY NOTES

The dual cultural influences of France and Germany in Alsace were also reflected in Waldteufel's own background. The composer's mother came from Bavaria, Germany, and though his father was French, the family name is German. It bears little relation, however, to Waldteufel's entertaining music: Waldteufel translates as "Wood Devil."

SERGEI PROKOFIEV *1891–1953*

Lieutenant Kijé

OPUS 60: TROIKA

*I*n this movement, the central character Lieutenant Kijé and his bride are riding in a *troika* (a Russian sleigh). Against a background of jangling sleigh bells, the main melody emerges from a nearby tavern. It is an old Russian song, and less than flattering to women: "A woman's heart is like an inn. All those who wish go in." Prokofiev's music evokes a colorful picture of the troika speeding through a snow-filled Russian night.

DOUBLE FIRST

Prokofiev wrote the music for the proposed film *Lieutenant Kijé* in 1933. This was his first Soviet commission and his first film score. A year later he used sections of it for a five-movement suite. He also wrote an alternative version for solo baritone, that is rarely heard today.

KEY NOTES

For many, "Troika" is closely associated with Christmas. This is in part due to the 1975 pop record "Do You Believe in Father Christmas" by Greg Lake, which used this music as its theme. Ironically, the music was commissioned by an officially atheist state, and did not have any connection with Christmas!

ALEXANDER GLAZUNOV
1865–1936

The Seasons

OPUS 67, "WINTER": VARIATIONS 1–4 AND CODA

The general theme of "Winter" is characterized by a solo flute with gently fluttering strings accompanying. Glazunov gives winter four attributes: "Frost," "Ice," "Hail," and "Snow," each of which has a dance to itself. The variation for "Frost' is agile, represented by a woodwind theme over scurrying strings. "Ice" opens with a measured but sprightly tune played by clarinet and violas. "Hail" is accompanied by a side drum rattling throughout. The final variation, "Snow," features a waltz melody heard on the oboe. The coda is a faster section, light in character, which ends with repeated sweeps from the harp.

GLAZUNOV THE TASK MASTER

In 1905, Alexander Glazunov was appointed Director of the St. Petersburg Conservatory—a post he held for 25 years. He worked constantly to improve the standards of both staff and pupils, and would often show great concern for his students, among whom were Prokofiev and Shostakovich,

who went on to become two of the greatest Russian composers of the 20th century. Glazunov's administrative skills also helped steer the Conservatory through the Revolution in 1917, and ensured that it was granted special status as an educational institution. As if that weren't enough, he also continued to compose, founded an orchestra, and set up an opera studio.

Glazunov (left) *and the St. Petersburg Conservatory* (above), *which he served with great distinction.*

WHERE THE SEASONS BEGIN

Glazunov chose to commence his *Seasons* with "Winter" and to end with "Autumn." Vivaldi's cycle of violin concertos *The Four Seasons*, however, runs from "Spring" to "Winter." This is perhaps the more obvious, progressing from the joys of a new year to the coldness of its end. In Glazunov's music, by contrast, "Winter" is a magical, though desolate time, and the year reaches its close in the jubilation of the abundant harvest of "Autumn."

KEY NOTES

Tchaikovsky was also inspired by the seasons. The result was a set of 12 piano pieces, one for every month. Each has a subtitle, beginning with "By the Fire" for January. February is "Carnival" and March the "Song of the Lark," while December, the final piece, is predictably entitled "Christmas."

PYOTR TCHAIKOVSKY *1840–1893*

Symphony No.1 in G Minor

OPUS 13: WINTER DAYDREAMS

Although this is not intended to be descriptive music—Tchaikovsky was setting out to write his debut symphony along conventional classical lines—it remains powerfully evocative of a severe Russian winter landscape, in keeping with its poetic title. Indeed, the opening two movements to the work are subtitled "Daydreams on a Wintry Road" and "Land of Gloom, Land of Mists." However, this finale, despite a somber beginning, is a far jollier affair with the melody of an old Russian folk song—"I'm sowing a few flowers, my baby"—popping up several times as the movement builds to a powerful conclusion.

RUBINSTEINS TO THE RESCUE

When he started on his *Symphony No.1*, Tchaikovsky's confidence was at a low ebb. As part of his graduation diploma from the St. Petersburg Conservatory, he had been commissioned to write a cantata based on Schiller's "Ode to Joy" (the inspiration for the last movement of Beethoven's *Symphony No.9*). However, the nervous Tchaikovsky failed to turn up for the public performance of the cantata and the work was savaged by both the Conservatory's director, Anton Rubinstein (*left*), and the composer César Cui. Rubinstein, however, saw the young composer's potential and, as well as awarding the diploma, arranged for Tchaikovsky to work for his brother, Nikolai Rubinstein, (*right*) at the recently formed Moscow Conservatory.

SOLITARY LAUGHTER

While the inner turmoil that would play such a major part in Tchaikovsky's life had already begun to surface in 1866, there were periods when the composer was able to escape into a happier world. He often visited the large library at the Moscow Commercial Club where he entertained himself with the novels of Charles Dickens (*left*). He found *Pickwick Papers* particularly funny. However, his claim that: "There's no one to hear me, and the thought that no one hears me laughing makes me enjoy myself all the more" gives a truer insight into his frame of mind.

KEY NOTES

Tchaikovsky's efforts to write his First Symphony brought him to the brink of nervous collapse. He was so unhappy with the original version that he revised it twice before being satisfied.

Credits & Acknowledgments

PICTURE CREDITS

Cover /Title and Contents Pages/IBC
The Stock Market:
AKG London: 3(bl), 10(bl), 15(tr), 23(br);
Bridgeman Art Library, London/Giraudon/Galleria
Querini-Stampalia, Venice (Gabriele Bella: The
Frozen Lagoon) 2, British Library, London (George
Scharf: Winter in Germany) 12, Johnny Van Haeften
Gallery, London (David Vinckboons: The Blind
Hurdy Gurdy Player) 13(tr), Roy Miles Gallery,
London (Joseph Farquharson: Glowed with Tints of
Evening Hours) 16, New York Historical Society (C.
Parsons: Winter on the Skating Pond in Central
Park) 18, Forbes Magazine Collection, New York
(John Mongels Culverhouse: Napoleon III & the
Empress Eugenie Skating in the Bois de Boulogne)
20(bl), Private Collection (P. Eyrmakof: Troika Ride)
21, Ex-Edward James Foundation, Sussex (Giuseppe
Arcimboldo: Winter) 22, Victoria & Albert
Museum, London (William Powell Frith: Portrait of
Charles Dickens) 25(bl); E.T. Archive: 17(bl); Mary
Evans Picture Library: 3(tr), 5(bl), 6, 7(br), 8,
15(bc), 19(tr); Getty Images:11; Images Colour
Library: 24; Lebrecht Collection: 7(tl), 10(tr), 13(bl),
15(tl), 17(tl), 19(br & cl), 23(tr), 25(cr & tl);
Performing Arts Library/Clive Barda 4; Society for
Cultural Relations with the USSR: 5(tr), 9(bl); The
Stock Market: 9(tr), 14, 20(tr).

All illustrations and symbols: John See